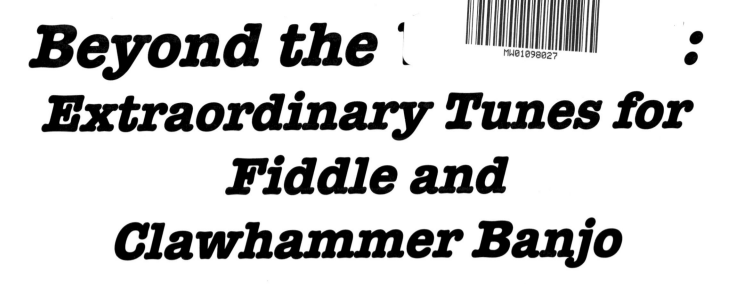

Beyond the 1 : Extraordinary Tunes for Fiddle and Clawhammer Banjo

by Dan Levenson

Cover photo courtesy of Dan Levenson Old Time Music.
Pictured in cover photograph: Dennis Russell, Dan Levenson and Jennifer Levenson

Dedication

The music business is a difficult way to make one's living but that is what I have done full-time for over twenty years now. It requires the support and encouragement of everyone around you, especially your family. I find myself among many *families* and thank all of you for that support over the years:

My immediate family with my wife, Jennifer Levenson, who has been a true inspiration, partner and rock of support as I make the journey called life on my musical path. We have been many places together and hope to go many more.

My extended family of my children and their families.

My parents - long passed - who raised me in a household filled with music.

My musical family of co-performers, players, jammers, listeners, and students.

To the Mel Bay Publications family and workers there who make my books available to you and give my musical writings voice to the world.

To my family of readers who love the music for what it is.

And finally, to Clifford Hardesty, Les Raber and all of those musicians now passed-on, who inspired us and entrusted us with their tunes to keep old-time music alive for another generation.

All tunes are traditional and in the public domain except

"Elkins"— by Larry Unger and Eden MacAdam-Somer ©2006
"Tippin' Back the Corn"— by Jordan Wankoff ©1996

Which are both used with the composers' permission.

Table of Contents

Introduction

Welcome to *Beyond the Waterfall: Extraordinary Tunes for Fiddle and Clawhammer Banjo*. It has been some 15 years since I wrote my first book, *Buzzard Banjo – Clawhammer Style* containing 25 tablature transcriptions. I originally self-published that book in a copy shop with comb binding and line art card-stock paper cover. It was my first book ever, and even though I had to learn to write tablature in order to produce it, folks have told me that they were (& are) amazed at how playable and truly musical those early tabs were.

That book was soon picked up by Mel Bay Publications and released with the original tabs plus the added reference CD with both a slow and up-to-speed version of each tune. That edition also added a nice glossy cover with a photo of me that was taken by my younger son, Joshua. That was in the year 2000. It has been a long road since then. Bill Bay said at the time that he would like to be the publisher for any future books I might want to write and to this day, he and his company have stood by that offer and have led me to this, my 14th publication with Mel Bay. Thank you Bill! Thank you Mel Bay Publications!

I am also indebted to Richard *"Bubba Hutch"* Hutchison for taking the time to teach me to write tab and keeping watch over me while I did those first transcriptions while visiting him at his home then in Houston, Texas. Bubba Hutch had been transcribing my playing from cassette recordings and sending them to *Banjo Newsletter* magazine for publication for several years. It was his lead and encouragement that made that first book happen. He passed away a few years ago and I can tell you he is missed. In some way, it is his spirit that has kept me transcribing this music for you as I continue to produce books with Mel Bay Publications. I also currently write and edit "Old Time Way" for *Banjo Newsletter* – their quarterly insert dedicated to old-time banjo playing.

As I look over the writing of my other 13 books currently in print, I have been fascinated by the development of both the style of transcriptions and my playing. It's gone from a single line of tablature to the current format where I provide standard notation as well as basic and advanced lines of tablature, offering you more choices and insight of what to play. I still wish I could provide more *music* for you as opposed to just more notes. BUT, that is what YOUR development is supposed to be all about. And while many folks *"poo-poo"* written sources saying that the old-timers didn't read, write or use written music, I can only tell you that virtually every home I entered, when meeting some of these older folks had written music in them even, if they didn't "play" from it. It is a tool like any other.

Like my past collections, this book is intended to be a tune repertoire book and not an instructional book. For that, I would direct you to my book *Clawhammer Banjo From Scratch* and the corresponding two DVD set, which are also available from Mel Bay Publications. My students have said this book is a must for anyone learning to play the clawhammer banjo style as well as anyone with a desire to improve their playing skills, no matter what level you currently play.

Likewise, though we had music classes even in public school and were taught the basics of music theory, I don't claim to be a "by-the-book" theorist when transcribing these tunes. If you wish to know more about time signatures, note values and things like that, please feel free to avail yourselves of the many books out there that competently explain music theory.

About the Title and Tune Selection

This book, *Beyond the Waterfall: Extraordinary Tunes for Fiddle and Clawhammer Banjo* presents another 40 tunes for you to play for fun and profit! If you are reading this book you are probably able to competently play tunes like *Over the Waterfall* as well as innumerable other old-time standards such as *Forked Deer, Soldier's Joy,* and *Mississippi Sawyer.* But, how many times can you play *Arkansas Traveler* without wishing that the tune would travel off to Arkansas never to return, and *Soldier's Joy* just isn't a joy anymore! Or perhaps you just like more esoteric and lesser known tunes that everyone else doesn't play. Yes, those standards of the old-time jam are great tunes, but you are ready for more. You are *SO OVER the waterfall* that you are now *BEYOND* the waterfall, so I have selected tunes for this book that should challenge and entertain you for some time to come.

The tunes in this volume are more of the less-often-played variety. Some are crooked, others, as we say – *eat their own tail* and start over before you realize they have ended. Still others are interesting tunes that, while popular with the folks in the old-time community, are not often played at jam sessions – especially at more, shall we say, user-friendly jams. Some might not even be considered old-time by everyone, but sure are fun to play!

I have also included several more popular songs along with their words. Singing has always been part of the old-time tradition. In recent years, it has been sidelined, but can still be enjoyed at some gatherings. Here are a few to try out where they are welcome.

So enjoy this eclectic collection of old-time tunes. They may be a bit more work than the standards, but I think you'll agree they are worth it!

Listen, Listen, Listen

You may have already noticed that there are no recordings to accompany this book – at least not yet. Mel Bay has opted to stop including recordings with their books primarily due to the cost of providing a physical CD with the publication. Also, not to be ignored, is the time it adds to getting a volume such as this to you. But I have a couple of other reasons for you to consider. First, the primary mantra I believe in when learning any style of music is, *"Listen, listen, listen,"* and I am not just referring to the literal interpretation of the transcriptions in this book. If you don't hear it, you will not be able to play it and have it sound like old-time music. I want to encourage you to find these tunes as played by others as well as my rendering of them. While I hope to eventually provide both audio and video recordings of my playing these tunes, at the moment I feel you should go out of your way to find multiple recorded versions of these tunes in order to get the *flavor* as well as the literal playing of them. In addition, my version is my version and, while I strive here to make sure you have options, these versions may not be the ones others play or those you prefer. I consider myself *A* source for these but not *THE* source — an unusual admission, I'll confess. In the long run, I want you to play the tunes like, well, you, but still be able to adapt and fit-in when playing with others.

To help you accomplish that goal I have provided a starting source for most of them, and today the Internet can easily provide others. The sources I provide are usually the oldest versions I could find (always my preferred starting point), or – in the case of the few more modern tunes – the composer's website or a list of versions I know to exist. In each case, consider these the start of your journey to understand and more competently play these tunes, not the final authority. Consider it a good way to start or augment your old-time music collection and your mental image of the tunes it contains.

About the Format

Most of the tunes and songs presented here have the following components:

Tune Title – One tune can have many names! The most commonly known name for the tune is in **bold** text. I also list other common names as aka's (also known as) in plain text.

Tuning – I have listed the banjo tuning to reflect the tuning used for the banjo tablature. I have not noted capo use, so if you use one, please remember that for the key of A (A tuning – aEAC#E) you would tune the banjo to G tuning (gDGBD) then put your capo at the second fret and tune, capo or spike your fifth string up to a. For D (aDADE) you would likewise tune to C (gCGCD) and capo at the second fret and adjust the fifth string as above.

No fiddle tuning is noted since the standard notation is written to reflect the standard tuning of a fiddle (GDae low to high strings). HOWEVER, many fiddlers, including myself, use a variety of tunings – often called *cross tuning* for playing in keys such as A or D. For most A tunes, I tend to use AEae cross tuning and AEac# (aka Calico Tuning) for some others. Likewise many folks use ADae for most of their D tunes which allows for a good unison C# note on the G (now A) string with the third finger instead of the pinky.

I feel the tunes and instrument sound better that way, so you might want to give it a try but remember if you do, you will have to transpose the notes below A on the main staff to reflect that change.

Chord Line - The chord names are printed above the standard notation line at each chord change and at the beginning of each part. Chords are not so intuitive or fixed as most folks would believe and are therefore often in dispute. I use the "don't encourage bad music" rule. Just because the old timers might not have known a better chord doesn't mean theirs was the best choice or that it sounded good. Use your judgment here as in all music. Use what you like, like what you use. I like mine but fully acknowledge there are other, perhaps better options.

Fiddle Melody – This is the line folks playing fiddle (or other melody instruments) would follow. Unlike past books this version is a fairly well developed melody line including suggested note combinations (slurs), selected double stops and drones. It is a starting point for deriving the tab and while developed, it is not necessarily indicative of all the possible choices you could make in playing these tunes. The melody line is intended to be an accessible reference point but not a master that is slavishly reproduced by the tab. It's more than a good skeleton or basic starting point, but far from a comprehensive *final* arraignment.

Song Lyrics – I have included the words to several popular old time songs with the first verse included as it would be sung within the body of the score. More verses are included after the score, with the understanding that you would change the rhythmic structure as the words of the verses dictate.

Basic Banjo Tablature – This line will *usually* be playable by all but the most beginning players, though that will not *always* be the case. While it is intended to be more basic than the advanced or lead line, it is not an overly simplified version of the tune. These versions should at least follow the basic melody of the tune, even if it is not fully melodic. Sometimes, the basic version just isn't going to be that easy! (Note that in songs – tunes with words – this line will be listed as back-up or song accompaniment and is the line you would use to keep a rhythmic flow going while you sing the tune.)

Advanced Banjo Tablature - This line should provide more of a challenge to almost everyone. It will require more time and finesse as it is more *ornamental* (more than just *melodic*) and may include some less than intuitive ways of playing some passages. It still surprises me to see some of my fingering written out in tablature. This version is pretty much the most intricate rendition of the tune, as it contains more hammer-ons, pull-offs, and double and drop thumbs.

This line may or may *NOT* agree with the basic and standard notation lines. That is partly because of other techniques used, including counter melody, blue notes and syncopation. You can also expect to find hammer-ons and pull-offs to open strings and what is commonly referred to as the *Galax lick*, which is indicated by a full-beat drawn-out finger stroke followed by a full-beat-long thumbed note. (Again, in *songs* – tunes with lyrics – this line will be listed as the *melodic lead* line and is what you would play between sung verses.)

About Written Music

Please remember that written music has many limitations when it comes to accurately representing true *music*. There are many subtleties and inflections that cannot really be represented by the limited palette that written music provides. Also, in one written pass through any tune, there are countless variations of notes and techniques that likely would not ALL be played in one pass through the tune. This is done so you have as many options as possible to choose from when you play the tune. Learn the written music, but listen to recorded versions, too. Find older (I often look for the oldest) sources whenever you can. If you listen long enough, you will find that you can sing the tune before you ever try to play it which brings me to:

Creativity - Beyond The *Right* (Write) way - My version will not be the only one you will come upon as you journey through the old time music world. These versions of the tunes come from how I hear and play music that has been handed down for generations and has been CHANGED for many reasons by every player who has handled and played each tune. Mine are not supposed to be the only ones you always want to play or hear. You get to put your own variations in as well. A and B parts may be one way here, and reversed in your jam session. Some folks may play only one A and others two. Tune titles may vary. You may want to make a crooked tune* come out even for a dance or make an even tune crooked to win a contest or impress friends.

These transcriptions are intended to be a starting point, not an ending. In reality, there is no one right way to play any of these tunes. Everything is open to your interpretation. If there is a right way it is the way you like it. *HOWEVER*, if you are going to play with others - a goal of most but not all folks - then the right way will be the one you agree on in your group no matter how large or small. With more licks in your bag of tricks, you will be better able to adapt to the music of the day and time.

* A *crooked tune* is any tune that does not follow the 32 bar – A part of 8 bars repeated followed by a B part of 8 bars repeated – tune total count instead having an un-even number of bars, parts or notes within them.

Reading the Tablature

The banjo lines in this book are written in a type of music notation known as *tablature*. For fretted instruments, reading tablature is in many ways easier than reading music. In tablature the lines of the staff indicate the strings of the banjo and the notes are numbers that tell you the fret numbers on each string.

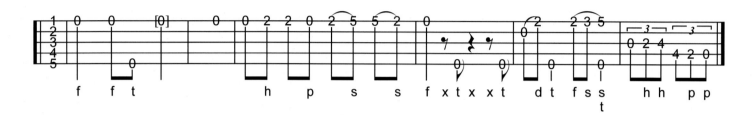

In the tablature example above, the top line of the staff represents the first string of your banjo and the bottom line the 5th (short) string. The second measure of the example above shows some of the types of notes used. A quarter note counts as 1 beat (say, "one"). Eighth notes count as 1/2 beat each so, 2 eighth notes = one quarter note (say, "one and") and a half note counts for 2 beats or 2 times a quarter note (say, "one, two"). The next measure shows a whole note, which counts as 4 beats (say, "one, two, three, four"). A dot (˙) next to the note adds half the value of the note to the time of that note (i.e. a quarter note is one beat, a quarter note followed by the dot is one and a half beats).

The letters under the note symbols will indicate whether you use the finger - "f" or the thumb - "t" of your right hand to play the note. An "x" indicates silence and means that you don't sound the note here. Your hand keeps moving down and up even though you are not sounding a note.

The h, p and s give playing directions for your left hand. The "h" is the symbol for a hammer-on, the "p" is the symbol for a pull-off and the "s" indicates a slide. I also use a "slur" (the curve above the notes) for the slide. Notes with no marking under them should fit the rule that if the note is on the first half of the beat, it is played with your finger. If on the second half of the beat, it is played with your thumb or is a hammer-on, slide, or pull-off.

The Galax Lick – This name is the common name given to a move where you actually roll across two beats with the finger and thumb where each gets a full beat instead of the usual half beat for each. Your finger plays the first notes of the series with the down stroke of your hand in a delayed motion taking a full beat. It can be a single note, a hammer on or slide on that string or it might require you to drag ("d") the finger stroke across the multiple strings – then with a continued motion as your hand circles back up the thumb plays the fifth string. That puts the fifth string sounding at the beginning of the second beat instead of the end of the first one. You are actually taking 2 beats to complete the down-up hand motion of clawhammer playing instead of the usual one beat. Two types of this lick are shown in the next to last measure of the example above.

Triplets – The last measure in the example shows what are called *triplets*. Triplets are three notes played in the space of two notes. In this case it is 3 eighth notes. They are indicated by that little broken bracket with the 3 set in it. You play it by striking the first note followed by two hammer-on's, pull-offs or some combination of those in a row.

A Final Note of Encouragement

There are no mistakes, only notes you didn't intend to play. If you find you played a note or phrase differently from the written music and you like it, cool. If you play a note you don't like, well, don't play that one next time.

Music is to be enjoyed by all and meant to express your soul. Don't be afraid to play it your way, but don't be reluctant to experiment or try someone else's version either.

Play alone or play together.

Whatever you choose and your community or musical partner agree on is fine. Just...

Play Nice!

Ask That Pretty Girl to Be My Wife

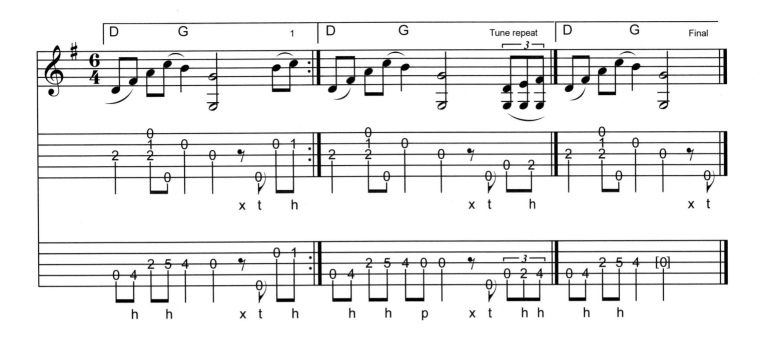

Most everyone traces this one back to the playing of Clyde Davenport. I met Clyde at the Tennessee Banjo Institute in 1988 where he said, "Dan, the banjo players job is to follow the fiddler note for note." And that's a quote! Do your best with this one. Phew!

As to the chords, as usual use your judgement. You may feel the C chord in the B part could come a measure earlier, or leave it out all together. The D chord in the last measure could also be left out if you like a more minimalist approach to chording.

Been All Around This World

aka Hang Me

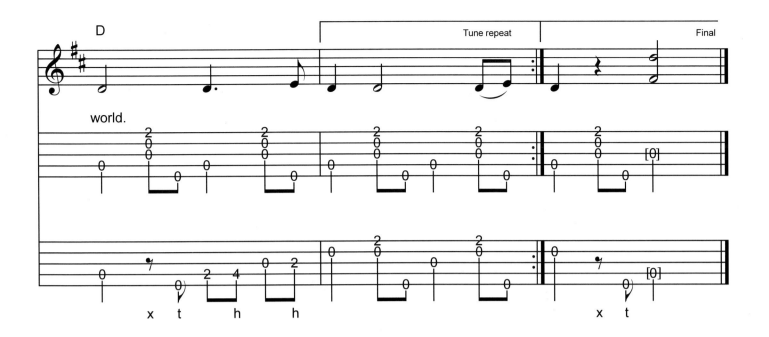

world.

There are SO many versions of this tune, but it seems to date back to the 1870's hanging of an outlaw ordered by Issac Charles Parker – the "hangin' judge" in Fort Smith, Arkansas. The most known modern versions were done by The Highwoods Stringband and, believe it or not, The Grateful Dead!

Here are a few of the most popular verses, which are collected from various sources and finessed by what I remember and sing. The "Hang me..." verse is often used as a chorus between verses.

Hang me, oh hang me, I'll be dead and gone (x2)
It's not the hangin' that I mind, it's waitin' in the jail so long
Lord, lord, I've been all around this world.

Up on the Blue Ridge mountain, there I'll take my stand (x2)
A rifle on my shoulder, a pistol in my hand
Lord, lord, I've been all around this world.

Lulu, my Lulu, come and open up the door (x2)
Before I have to open it with my old forty-four
Lord, lord I've been all around this world.

I went to work on the railroad, boys, the mud up to my knees (x2)
The boss come round to boss me, boys, I done just as I pleased
Lord, lord, I been all round this world.

Bring to me my supper boys, I'll eat her done or raw (x2)
For I haven't had a square meal since I left Arkansas
Lord, lord, I've been all around this world.

Mama and papa, little sister makes three (x2)
They're coming in the morning, to see me on the gallows tree
Lord, lord, I've been all around this world.

Been to the East, Been to the West

Banjo - gDGBD

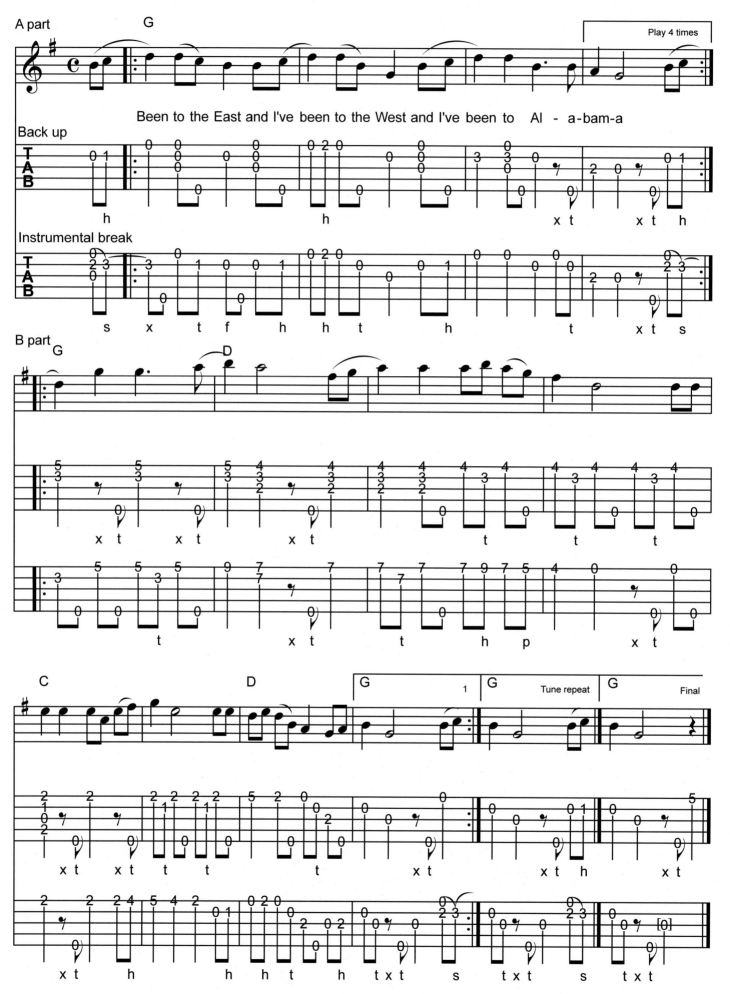

Been to the East and I've been to the West and I've been to Al - a-bam-a

14

This one comes from the playing of the Leake County Revelers about 1927 or 28.

While it does have words like a good song should, I consider it to be one of those *fiddle tunes with words* as opposed to a true "song" but hey, we'll take it! It's a great tune and one where you can throw out the words and not have to think too hard!

Oh, and according to a search of the Internet, a *yellowhammer* is actually another name for the Northern Flicker – the state bird of Alabama. There is another bird which is considered to be the *real* yellowhammer. It's actually a bird in the bunting family which is native to Eurasia! You can imagine the leg of either one would be pretty "bad for to eat!" as the original words said.

The Revelers played the first part 3 times and the second part only once. Most folks today play it more danceable by todays "rules" so would play that short A part 4 times and the B part twice giving you a 32-bar tune structure preferred by today's contra dance callers. Square dance callers likely wouldn't care, but then – they wouldn't want you to sing!

Been to the East and
I've been to the West, and
I've been to Alabama.

Oh the worst darn thing
I ever for to eat,
Was the leg of the yellowhammer.

(original verse for above:)
Oh they gave me something
bad for to eat,
was the leg of the yellowhammer.

Prettiest girl
I ever did see
She lives in Alabama

Wanna know her name
I'll tell you what it be
Her name was Susiana

Blackjack Grove

Banjo - aEAC#E

16

I'm not sure exactly where or when I first heard this tune but it is one of my favorites and way underplayed in the jam world today. This one is definitely worth the work and *extraordinary* in so many ways!

According to Bruce Greene the title refers to a grove of blackjack oak trees (Quercus marilandica) which are a member of the red oak family.

One of the most interesting parts of this tune is that slide from the G to the G# which happens on the high E string and the C natural to C# on the A string. I indicate the slide with an "s" under the sharped notes.

Old recordings of this tune include Kentucky fiddlers Walter McNew and Art Stamper who can both be heard on *The Digital Library of Appalachia.*

Blue-Eyed Susie

Banjo - gDGBD

Yes, BLUE eyed. This one is a tune from the repertoire of Elmo Newcomer of Pipe Creek, TX and collected by Howard Rains and Trish Spencer. You can hear it on their recording *The Old Texas Fiddle Vol. II.*

Some may consider the D part just a variant of the C part.

Also in the D part, first measure, some (many? lol) may consider the F# under the D notes to be too discordant for their taste, so the parenthesis means that you can leave them out. Of course all double stops and bowings are merely suggestions anyway, but...

Likewise the chords you may hear and prefer may differ from mine. Some folks may try adding a D chord in the second part of the first and third measures and a C chord in the second part of the second and fourth measures of the A part. I don't think it is necessary nor does it add to the character of the tune so I didn't write it in. (GDGC GDGC) You get to choose.

19

Chattanooga

aka Old Chattanooga

Banjo - gDGBD

20

This one is fun and not often played at jams. I think it should be played more. A couple of notes though on what makes this one unique. Note the syncopation in measures 3, 7, 12 & 16. Take time to get that right as to me, it is one of the coolest parts of the tune. You can choose to play the tune without it (as I wrote it in the basic banjo line), but I feel it strips much of the character from the tune.

Also, the Em chord in the B part is something that can be used instead of the C chord in the A part and likewise if the minor bothers you; use the C instead of the Em in the B part. Also, some folks substitute the last four measures of the A part for the last 4 measures of the B part. A nice variation you might want to try

I can't really say where I first heard it. Written references include the (Stacy) *Phillips Collection of American Fiddle Tunes* and it is also referenced in the *Millner-Koken* collection with a recording by Blaine Smith. Both reference it under the name *Chattanooga*. Recorded versions include The Haints on their recording *Sheeps And Hogs Walking Through The Pasture* as well as a version by Harry Bollick & Ken Blume on their *That Banjo From Hell* CD. Harry and Ken strive remain faithful to the older versions of the tune.

Chinquipin Hunting

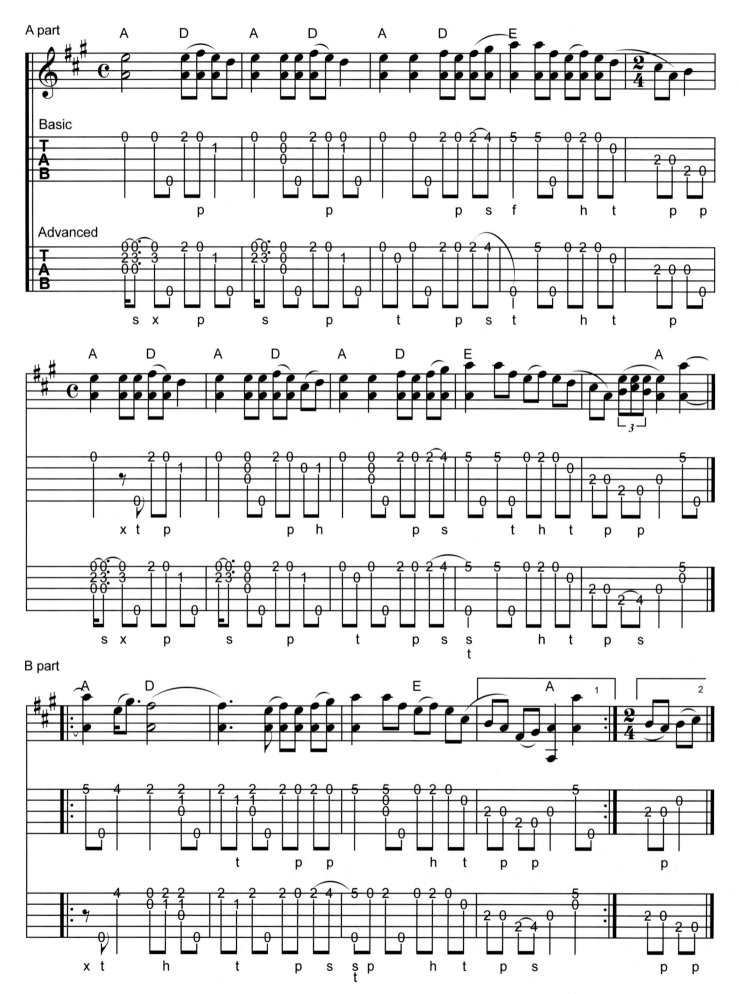

22

The advanced banjo tab should give banjo players a syncopation workout!

This one can be confusing because there are several tunes that appear under this same name; this tune is also referred to simply as "Chinquapin" as an alternate name, AND there is another tune named "Chinquapin" as well – just to add to the confusion.

The one transcribed here is based on the version The Hellbenders play on their self-titled recording. I'd like to find an older source recording, but at this moment in time - I have not. I'll keep looking though!

This tune was in heavy jam rotation some years ago, but seems to have either fallen out of favor or is beyond the level of most of today's basic jammers. Either way, it is a great one to have in your repertoire.

There is some debate as to which part to end on and while I have chosen to end it on the C part, many folks go back as though starting the tune and end it on the A part. You choose. Just make sure all of you are on the same page so to speak.

Dusty Miller

24

This is another interesting tune and one worth the effort it takes to play it well. While it seems simple in sound, the bowing and movement of the melody notes will take some work to get it to flow.

Banjo players will find that there is really no logical way to play all of the notes of the tune let alone play it in the same register (octave) but then, you are the banjo player. The melody is not really your responsibility. That is for the fiddlers. So get as many as you can (or want to) but timing is going to be important too.

Both of the recordings I have of this version of *Dusty Miller* (and there are a bunch of tunes by that name) are more modern recordings – one from Lynn "Chirps" Smith and the other from a West Virginia band comprised of Jerry Milnes, Dave Bing, Ron Mullennex, Mark Payne and Jim Martin on their *Gandydancer* recording.

Elkins

A dancing concertina player at our Monday night jams asked me if I knew this one last fall, but I didn't. I looked it up and got varied input from some of the other musicians in the area who did. I even got a video of it being played at the big Winfield music festival by Larry and Eden and I was HOOKED! I love this tune! It is a staple at our jams now.

While the arrangement is mine, it includes the Bm chord in the B part as in Larry's original version which I maintain here in this rendition. Like always, choose to use this chord or leave it out. I think it adds something extra.

Larry says, "This tune was written (in about 15 minutes) in a band workshop I was leading... there were about 6 of them (in the class) who each put in a measure or two."

Contact Larry about his music and his band Notorious to hear this tune and more from this skilled modern writer of traditional music. His site is http://www.larryunger.net/

Flying Clouds

aka Flying Cloud Cotillion

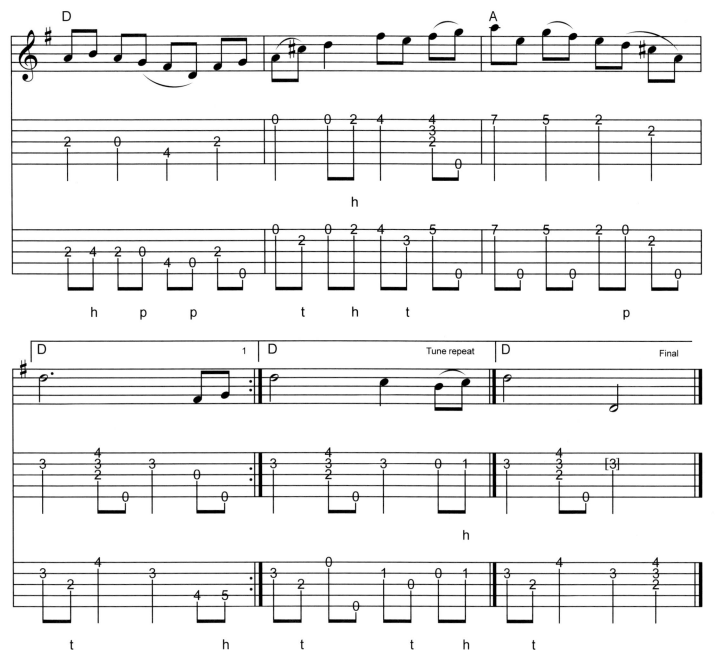

This one goes way back to Charlie Poole and his North Carolina Ramblers days! You start out in the key of G but then the tune switches to the key of D for the B part. (Charlie played it in F and C! Feel free to give it a go.)

Banjo players will notice that the 5th string often sounds "out of tune" or not really *right* when you play the B part. That discord is one of the reasons many of the 5th-string notes in the B part have a "g" under them indicating what I call a *ghost note* because while you want the rhythmic sound of the 5th string, you touch that string but do not *clearly* sound it, giving you texture but not discord.

Play as much or as little of the 5th string as you feel comfortable with. Likewise, the banjo player is not really able to easily get all of the melody and much of what you can get is implied and somewhat discordant. To some, this is just part of the banjo mystique. To others, it is a difficult sound. If those notes sound louder than you want, so be it. Don't dwell on it just play through.

Fiddlers, note the C# in the B part, even though I didn't change the key signature in the score.

29

Flying Indian

I alter the chords as I please in this one. Sometimes I use the Em instead of any of the C chords; other times I go right to the D where the C appears in the A part, and towards the end of the second part. But, hey, you get to choose! Some folks never like to hear a minor chord because they think the old timers never used minor chords - which they did, but that can be a discussion for another book.

The B part can be played on fiddle in the lower register, giving the tune quite an earthy feel and allowing you avoid that high B note, which really takes some practice. I'm nailing it myself more often than not these days - LOL! So remember to mix it up.

The basic banjo version avoids high chords, by staying in the lower register and holding the basic chord shapes while playing a bum-did-dy or (my preference) a bum-pa-did-dy rhythm. It won't matter much which strings you hit that way as any string will be part of the chord.

Admittedly, this is a repeat tune from another of my books but it seems more developed to me and hence deserves another look. I didn't realize I had duplicated it until I had written it out again. I do hope y'all don't mind. SO many Indians – lost, flying, big, pretty; it gets hard to keep track of them all!

There are not many recordings of this one, but it was a Boiled Buzzards favorite that I got from Christian Wig. I recorded it on my *New Frontier* album some years ago. The oldest version I have is from Claris & Joe Shelor as part of *Old Originals Vol. 1* on Rounder Recordings.

Free Little Bird

Banjo - aDADE

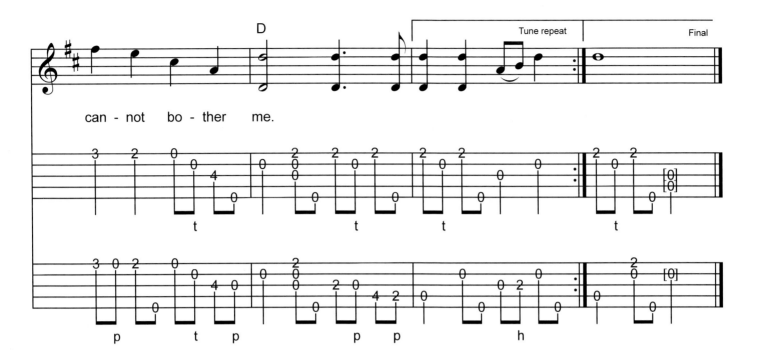

can - not bo - ther me.

Not to be confused with *Free Bird,* of course. This one's as old as the hills and as widely sung as any tune out there. Many of the verses are what are called *floating verses* as they appear in more than one song. For instance, most all the verses of *Mole in the Ground* will fit this melody and many are very close if not the same.

I'm as free a little bird as I can be, I can be. I'm as free a little bird as I can be,
I'll build my home in the weeping willow tree, where the bad boys, they cannot bother me.

I wish I was a little fish, a little fish. I'd never bite a hook or a line
I'd swim way out to the middle of the sea, and leave all them big fish behind.

I wish I was a birdy in the sky, in the sky. I wish I was a birdy in the sky,
If I was a bird in the sky, I would fly so high, and watch all the people on the ground.

I wish I was a mole in the ground, in the ground. I wish I was a mole in the ground
If I's a mole in the ground, I would root that mountain down, if I was a mole in the ground.

Carry me home little birdie carry me home. Carry me home little birdie, carry me home
Carry me home to my wife, she's the joy of my life, carry me home little birdie,
carry me home.

I'll never build my nest on the ground, on the ground. I'll never build my nest on the ground;
I'd build my nest in the white oak tree, where the bad boys can not tear me down.

I'd never steal the honey from a bee, from a bee. I'd never steal the honey from a bee,
But I'd steal me a kiss from my sweet darling's lips, and we'd fly away 'cross the sea.

I'm as free a little bird as I can be, I can be. I'm as free a little bird as I can be
I'm free at my age as a birdie in the cage, I'm as free a little bird as I can be.

Froggy Went a Courting

Banjo - gDGBD

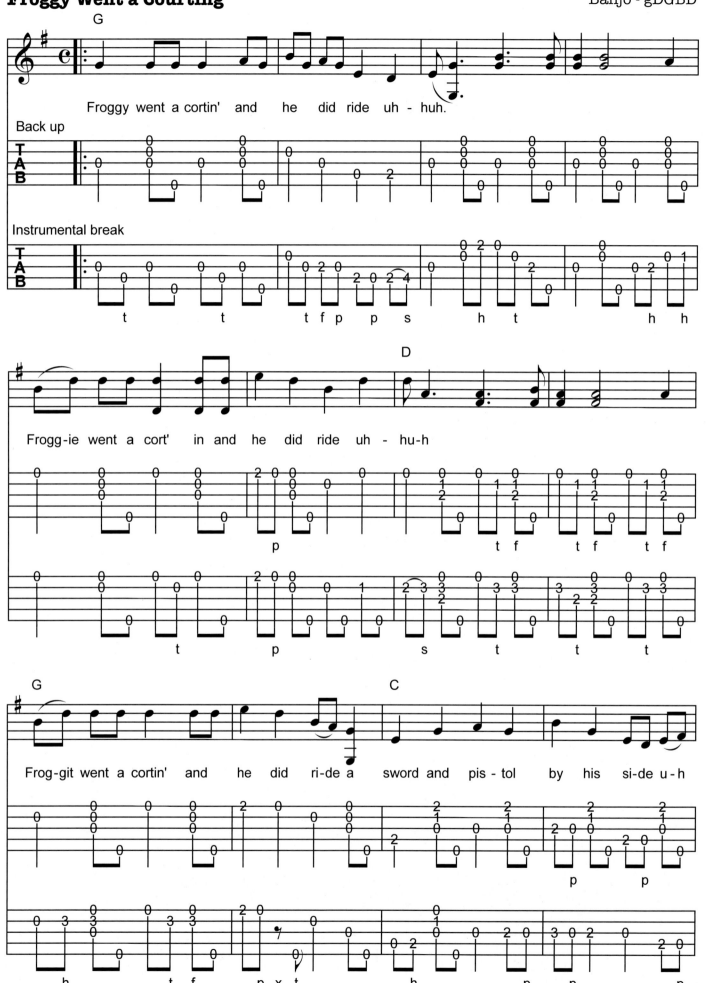

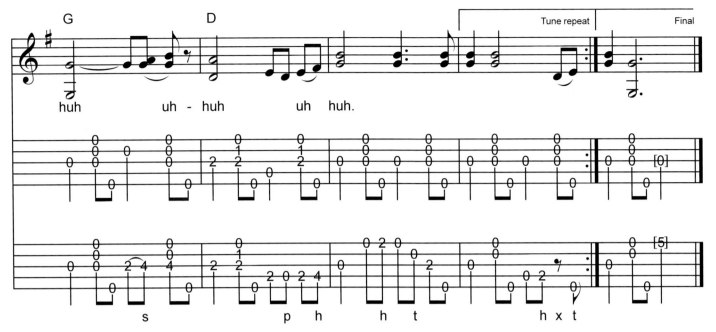

huh   uh - huh   uh huh.

I thought this one was a natural, and it was about time someone wrote it out. So many of us sang it when we were young. It's great for shows and hey, if you listen close the melody is a lot like *Policeman*. Who knew? Dating back to 1548, lyrics abound. There is a "modern" source version that dates back to 1923, but it's not particularly *sing-able* with those old words. SO the lyrics here are a more modern version based upon several others I have heard and sung over the years. And, you can add more because, as the song says, "If you want any more you can get it your self." Uh huh, uh-huh, uh-huh!

Froggy went a courtin and he did ride. Uh-huh. (x2)
Froggy went a courtin and he did ride. A sword and a pistol by his side Uh-huh, uh-huh, uh-huh.

He went down to Missie Mousie's door. Uh-huh. (x2).
He went down to Missie Mousie's door. He'd been there many times before. Uh-huh...

Took Missie Mouse upon his knee. Uh-huh. (x2).
Took Missie Mouse upon his knee, said, "Missie Mouse will you marry me?" Uh-huh, uh-huh, uh-huh.

Not without Uncle Rat's consent. Uh-huh. (x2).
Without Uncle Rat's consent, I wouldn't marry the president. Uh-huh, uh-huh, uh-huh.

Uncle Rat laughed and shook his sides. Uh-huh. (x2).
Uncle Rat laughed and shook his sides, to think his niece would be a bride. Uh-huh, uh-huh, uh-huh.

Where shall the wedding supper be? Uh-huh. (x2)
Where shall the wedding supper be? Way down yonder in a hollow tree, Uh-huh, uh-huh, uh-huh.

What should the wedding supper be?, Uh-huh (x3) Fried mosquito in a black-eyed pea, Uh-huh...

Well, first to come in was a flyin' moth, Uh-huh (x3) She laid out the table cloth, Uh-huh...

Next came in was a bumblebee, Uh-huh (x3) He danced a jig with a two-leg flea. Uh-huh...

Next to come in was Mrs. Cow, Uh-huh (x3) She tried to dance but she didn't know how, Uh-huh...

Next to come in was a big black snake, Uh-huh (x3) Ate up all of the wedding cake, Uh-huh...

They owls did hoot and the birds they sang, Uh-huh (x3) Through the woods the music rang. Uh-huh...

A little piece of cornbread layin' on a shelf, Uh-huh (x3) If you want any more, you can sing it yourself,
Uh-huh, uh-huh, uh-huh...

Get Off Your Money

Banjo - gCGCD

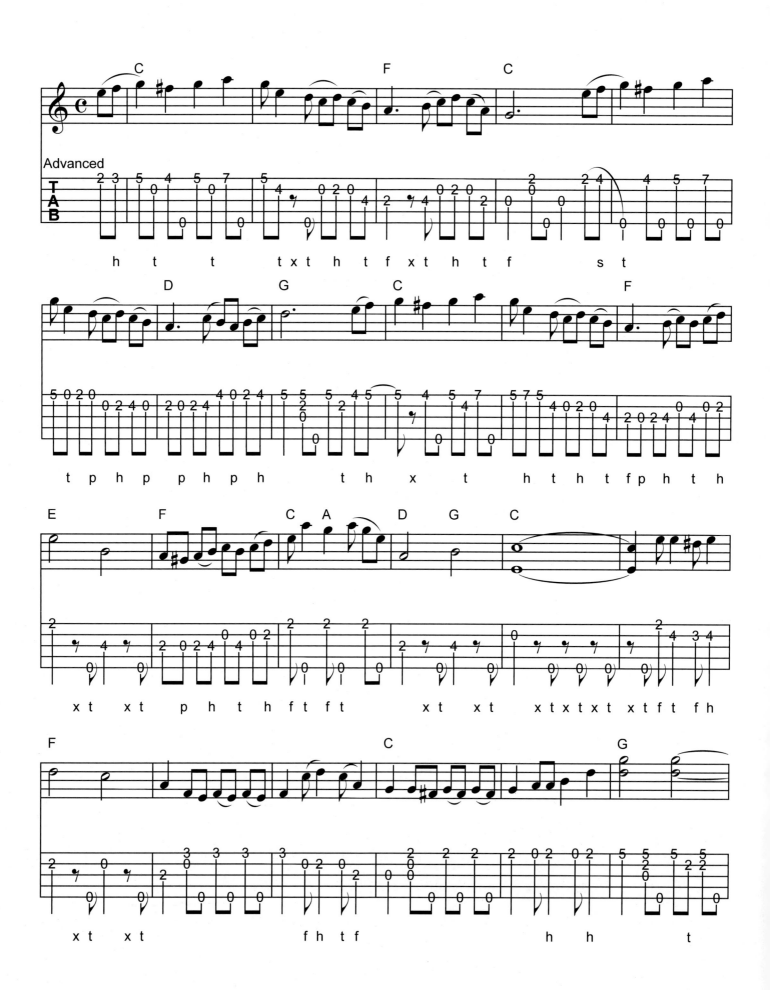

36

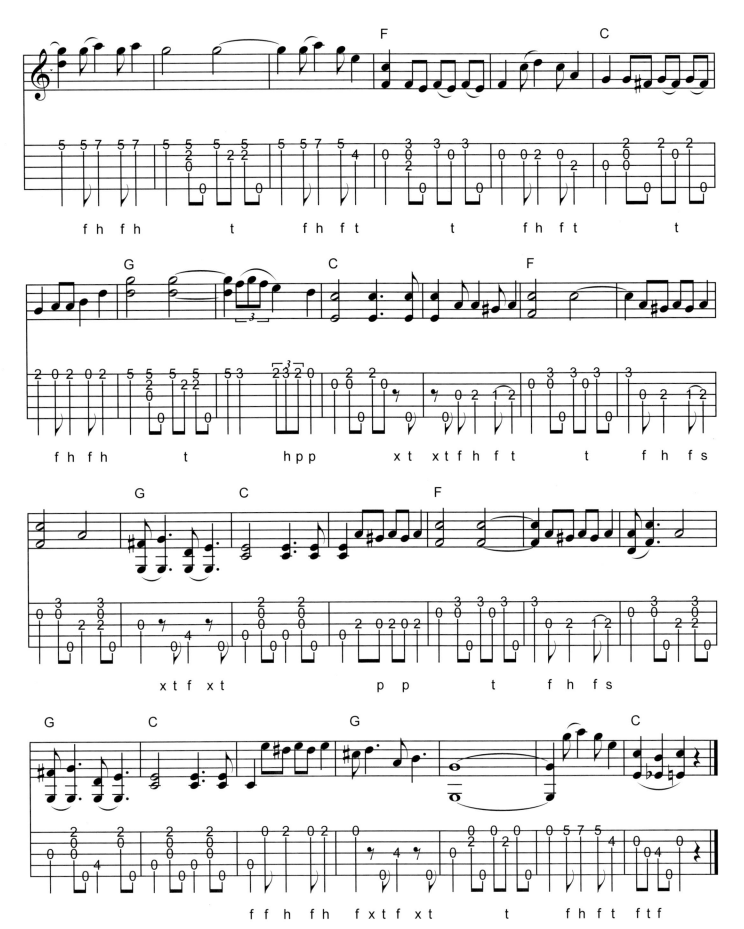

Here's a great old Stripling Brothers tune! Yes, not quite the way they played it but hey, make the changes you feel you need to make, but play this tune!

Only an advanced version here for banjo. Not an easy one for you banjo players, but lots of interesting right-hand fingering hence the mass of right-hand finger markings!

There is a wonderful and VERY complete history of this tune on the web but briefly stated, outside Missouri it is usually attributed to the playing of Charlie Walden who gets it from Pete McMahan of Columbia, Missouri. Evidently, *Gilsaw* is a family name and the name of a "tramp" fiddler who played the tune at the Wabash Railroad depot in Montgomery City (Montgomery County), ca. 1933-1935. The Gilsaw family's presence in the Columbia area dates back to the 1800's. Further discussion of "Gilsaw," together with a transcription, appears in Howard Marshall's book, *Fiddler's Dream* (Columbia, University of Missouri Press, 2016).

Pete McMahan, with Mickey Soltys playing guitar, was recorded in 1986 by Howard Marshall and Amy Skillman for the documentary recording, *Now That's a Good Tune* – a 1989 release of traditional Missouri fiddling produced by the University of Missouri, Columbia. The recording is currently available from Voyager Records and is well worth a listen, BUT *this* tune did not appear on that recording of so many of Missouri's great fiddlers.

The McMahan recording of "Gilsaw" can be heard on *Ozark Mountain Waltz* (MSOTFA cassette #001, 1987) and on the Slippery Hill website which references the *Millner-Koken Collection of American Fiddle Tunes*.

Glory Medley

This is a Texas tune from Howard Rains' recording *The Old Texas Fiddle* (Vol. 1). It comes from the playing of J.W. Whatley of Austin, TX. The title, "Glory Medley" is most likely "Glory Melody," with *medley* being JW's pronunciation of the word *melody*. So, while not a medley it sure is a great melody!

Banjo players: In the B part, 6th measure you see the "h*" for the hammer-on which is a hammer-on to an un-played string (also called an alternate string hammer-on). You could play the open first string along with the 1st fret on the second string if you like. That is most certainly up to you.

Fiddlers: I usually play this (and most all of my A tunes) in *A cross* tuning - fiddle tuned AEae low to high. That makes the drones here much easier to play and while I have written it in *standard* GDae tuning, it sounds much better in cross tuning. In addition, in cross tuning, you can more easily play the second part on the *low* strings using the same fingering as on the upper strings.

41

Goodbye My Little Darling

This waltz is one of those tunes where the rhythm in the written version is misleading. While you are seeing strings of eighth notes they would sound quite stiff and static if you played them with equal measure. SO, you have to *swing* the eighth notes it to make it sound right and give it that kind of a Louisiana – Texas, almost Cajun feel. In my music writing software, a *swing* setting of 75 gives you the right feel. Of course, the best way to understand this is to listen to a recording or two of the tune so you get the proper feel.

It is also *crooked* since the the A part has only 7 measures, so it cuts off and repeats before you expect it to. The written layout of the measures is just unreal, but it is danceable.

In the basic banjo part, I've put in a few more notes than you need for a rhythmic back up so if you prefer, just hang onto full chords and quarter-eighth-eighth — bum-did-dy-did-dy — away. Another unusual feature banjo players will notice in the advanced part is that you will have to start on the back (up) beat with your thumb for the first note.

My source for this is Howard Rains, who learned it from a recording of Mike Seeger, who learned it from a 1936 recording of Louis Propps made by Alan Lomax in Pleasanton, Texas.

Greasy Coat

Banjo - aEAC#E

I don't spit and I don't chew and I don't go with girls who do.
I don't drink and I don't smoke and I don't mess with a grea - sy coat.

44

Edden Hammons' version and the *Ship in the Clouds* recording by Andy Cahan, Laura Fishleder and Lisa Ornstein are my favorites of this one. There are several meanings for the term, *greasy coat.* It has been suggested the term refers to an unwashed fleece (i.e., still retaining the lanolin), a Confederate soldier's or priest's coat – worn, greasy and dirty from overuse, or perhaps a condom. The *greasy string* verse probably refers to a slippery fiddle string. And while all of the Hammons family members and the Ship in the Clouds folks all seem to play all parts today, most people leave the middle (B) part out. I think that's sad. It is cool and makes the tune distinct!

Many folks like to tune their banjo to the modal tuning (aEADE) but I don't find that necessary.

Additional verses to the one in the score:

I don't drink, and I don't smoke, and I don't mess with a greasy coat.
Jaybird whistle and the cat bird sing; Mash down harder on the greasy string.

My old lady is mad at me; 'Cause I won't drink ginger tea;
She is good, she is bad; She gives me the devil when she gets mad.

I don't kiss, and I don't tell, and all you sinners gonna go to hell
When I ride my horse to town, I see that man in a greasy gown.

Happy Hollow

46

This tune works best in Calico tuning (AEac#) but pretty well in A cross as well (AEae).

Calico tuning emphasizes the unison sound of the open C# string as a drone while playing the C# on the high A string for a very cool sound and haunting overtones.

If you do choose to retune for this tune, hold that C# string for the first two measures of the B part and you'll see what I mean.

My favorite version for this one? The Red Hots album, *The Red Hots*! Of course, they play it in the key of G. Banjo players just take off that ol' capo and stay down to good old G tuning if you want to play along with them.

Fiddlers? That would mean tuning your fiddle to GDgd for G cross or GDgb for G Calico.

SO there are a couple more challenges for those of you who want to make your extraordinary tunes MORE extraordinary!

High Yellow

48

A true classic from the playing of Henry Reed. Look him up and you will hear what I mean. He was one of the earliest influences on this generation of old-time musicians.

You can get recordings of all of Henry's tunes, collected by Alan Jabour as they say, "back in the day." You'll be glad you did!

Indian Corn

Banjo - gDGBD

A tune credited to an Illinois fiddler W.O. Ault (aka "Willie" Ault) for the book *Dear Old Illinois*. I first heard it on a jam session recording by the band *Bigfoot* who later went on to put it on their CD *I've Got a Bulldog*. It was one of those "I got to get my fiddle out and play along" tunes as soon as I heard it. Lynn "Chirps" Smith also recorded this tune under the title "Ol' Woodard's Tune" on the recording, *Folksongs of Illinois #2: Fiddlers* .

Fiddlers should really take the time to practice that bow rocking at the beginning of the second part. It is one of the characteristics that, to me, makes the tune.

Banjo players, take note of that last measure in the B part's tune repeat. That is indeed a hammer-on to an un-played string within that triplet!

John Hardy

John Har - d-y wa-s a des-perate lit - ltle man wh - o

Back up

Melodic break

carried - tw-o g-uns every day When he shot a -

man on_the West Vir - gin - ia line Yo - u ou-ghta seen Jo-hn Har - dy get-in' a -

52

way Lo-rd Lord   you ought to see John Har-dy get-tin a-

wa - y

This tune has a long and fascinating history dating back to the 1894 hanging of John Hardy. Here's a few more verses.

I never lied to my forty-four gun, And hit's never lied to me.
You skinned me when we were playin dice last week. Now we're as even as can be, poor boy.
Now we're as even as can be.

John Hardy got to the railroad bridge where he thought that he would be free
And up stepped the sheriff who took him by the arm, saying, "Johnny, come along with me poor boy,
Johnny come along with me."

Now he'd been to the east and he'd been to the west, he's traveled this whole world round
He's been to the river and been baptized, but now he's on his hangin' ground, Lord Lord
But now he's on his hangin ground.

They hung John Hardy on the following morn, They strung him way up in the sky.
The last words that poor John Hardy said, "I'll see you in that great bye and by Lord Lord
See you in that great bye and bye."

They dug his grave with a silver spade, gold chain to lower him down
His friends and relations all crowed around when they laid him in the cold cold ground poor boy
Laid him in the cold cold ground.

Johnny Walk Along With Your Paper Collar On

Banjo - gDGBD

54

This is a wonderful tune that I got from Howard Rains' recording *Old Texas Tunes Vol. II*. Howard collected it from the playing of Duck Wootan of Junction, Texas.

There are 2 B parts that each repeat. You can play either one repeated or go from one to the other (playing each B part once instead of twice) for a total 8-bar B part.

While the tune is old, the words are not native to this melody. One verse comes from another tune, and 2 verses were made up by Howard and friends.The words fit the A part.

Here are verses 2 and 3:

What ya gonna do when you've had your fun? Johnny walk along with your paper collar on, Johnny walk along with your paper collar on, Johnny walk along with your paper collar on.

Walk along John in the setting sun, Johnny walk along with your paper collar on Johnny walk along with your paper collar on, Johnny walk along with your paper collar on. (Everybody) *"WHOOO!!!..."*

Leavin' Home

aka Frankie and Johnny

Banjo - gCGCD

56

Leaving Home – aka Frankie and Johnny

This one's all about the words and the rhythm. I have written out the fiddle version as it would follow the singing in the first part of the first verse. With the second part (the repeat) which begins, "Frankie begged and pleaded..." the note values no longer fit all of the word values so it is up to you to decide which to play, the literal rhythm of the words, or a backing melody while one sings.

When you DO sing, you likely won't play the melody so your interpretation will be part of what makes this song your own. This, the version as I sing it, is based upon Charlie Poole's singing of Ren Sheild's 1912 telling of the infamous story of Frankie and Johnny.

Frankie and Johnny were sweethearts; they had a quarrel one day,
Johnny said he's leavin', said he's going away,
Going away to roam, never coming home.

Frankie begged and pleaded, "Oh Johnny, won't you stay,
Oh, my honey, I've done you wrong, but please don't go away."
And Johnny sighed while Frankie cried,

Chorus

"I'm going away, I'm going to stay, I'm never coming home.
Gonna miss me, honey, in the days to come,
When the winter wind begins to blow, the ground is covered up with snow.
Think of me, your gonna wish me back, your loving man.
You're gonna miss me honey in the days, they says to come."

Frankie said to Johnny, "Say, man, your time has come."
From underneath her silk kimono she drew a forty-four gun
These love affairs are hard to bear.

Johnny he fled down the stairway, "Now Frankie please don't shoot." but,
Frankie aimed that forty-four and the gun went root-toot-toot,
Old Johnny's dead, because he said...

Chorus

Send for your rubber-tired hearse, y'all send for a rubber-tired hack, to
Carry little Johnny to the graveyard 'cause I've shot him in the back
With my great big gun, when he went to run.

Send for a thousand policemen for to take me far away, and
Lock me up in the dungeon cell and throw the key away,
Ol' Johnny's dead, because he said,...

McMichen's Reel

That's Clayton McMichen of the Skillet Lickers y'all. aka Hog Trough Reel

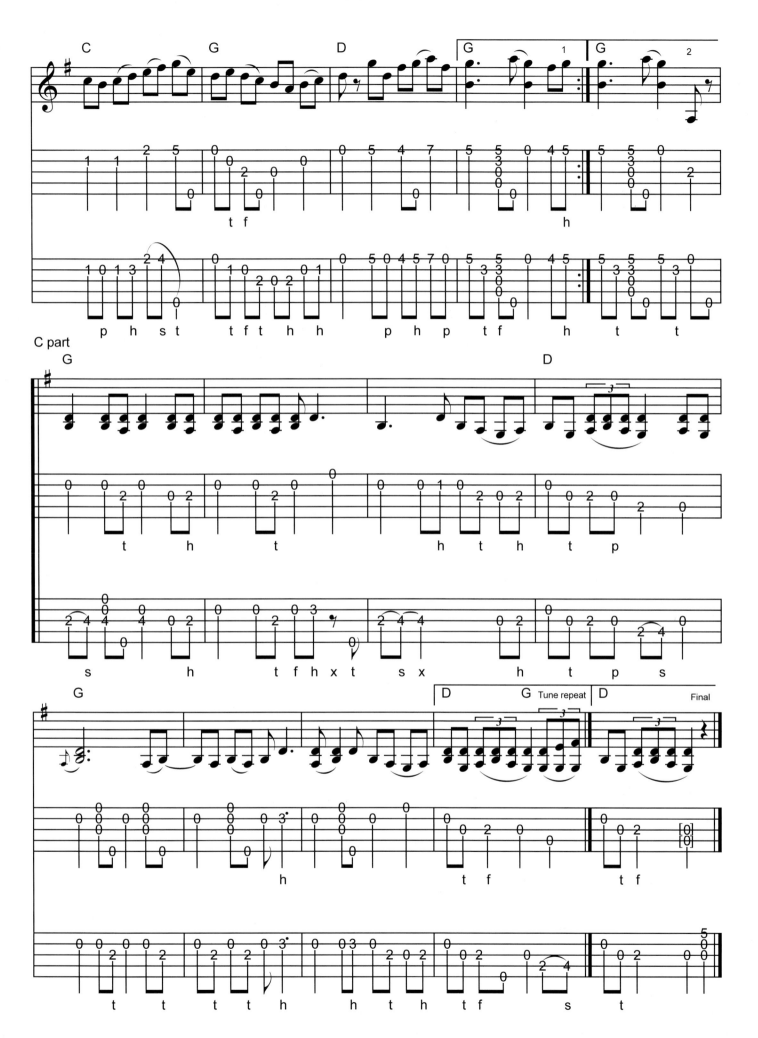

C part

61

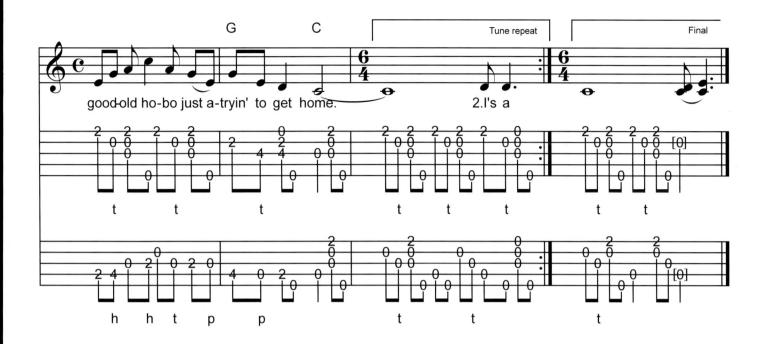

My version is based upon the playing and singing of Charlie Poole. Yes, he was a fingerpicker on the banjo but it's as old time as it gets. And there are extra beats in the 12th, 15th and 16th measures (makes them 6/4 time) to account for the hold when singing.

One chilly morning and it looked like rain; Round the corner come a passenger train
On the blind sat old Bill Jones; He's a good old hobo just a trying to get home.
Just a tryin' to get home, just a trying to get home
He's a good old hobo just a tryin' to get home.

I's way down Georgia on a tramp; Road's getting muddy and the leaves are getting damp
Got to hop me a freight train and leave this town
'Cause they don't like no hobos hanging around.
No hangin' around, no hangin' around
No they don't like no hobos hangin' around.

I left Atlanta one morning 'for day and the brakeman said, "son you gotta pay"
Ain't got no money so I pawned my shoes; I'm trying to get west I got the Milwaukee Blues.
Got the Milwaukee Blues, got the Milwaukee Blues
I'm just trying to get west I got the Milwaukee Blues.

Old Bill Jones said, "Before I die, won't ya fix the roads so the 'bo's can ride;
'Cause when they ride, they ride the rods, put their trust in the hands of G-d."
In the hands of G-d, In the hands of G-d
Put all their trust in the hands of G-d.

Old Bill Jones said, "Before I die, two more roads that I'd like to ride;"
Fireman said, "What can they be", "They's the Southern Pacific and the Santa Fe."
The Santa Fe, yes the Santa Fe
They's the Southern Pacific and the Santa Fe.

Old Bill Jones said, "Before I die, there's one more drink that I'd like to try."
Conductor said, "What can it be", "It's a glass of whisky with a cup of tea."
With a cup of tea, with a cup of tea
It's a glass of whisky with a cup of tea.

Old Bell Cow

Texas style!

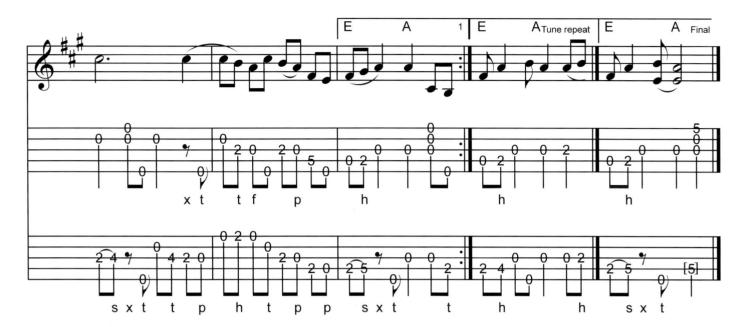

This is a cool Texas variant as played by Benny Thomasson. I've heard this variant before except for the third part, which seems to originate with Benny and makes it an even cooler tune. Most sources say this comes originally from the Dixie Crackers in 1928 or 29. One written source is *American Mountain Songs* by *Ethel Park Richardson*, published in 1927.

If you use the calico fiddle tuning as I suggest (AEac# low to high string) you can play the first two notes of the B part with a left hand pluck (pizzicato) instead of the bow. The pizzicato is indicated by the carrot (^) symbol above the notes in the score. In order to comfortably play the open A string drone in the first part you will have to go to calico.

Some of these days when I learn how,
I'm gonna milk that old bell cow.

CHORUS:
Oh, the bell cow, catch her by the tail,
Oh, the bell cow, milk her in the pail, (x2)

Partridge in the pea patch, pickin' up the peas,
Along comes the bell cow kickin' up her heels!

Went down to the cornfield to pick a mess of beans,
Along come the bell cow takin' after me.

The milk ain't whipped and the butter ain't fat,
The darned old cow ate my best hat.

I milked that bell cow and got a couple quarts,
Sold that milk and I got me a horse.

The bell cow has a couple a horns
Ain't been milked since I was born.

Way down yonder in Arkansas
The bell cow hoofed (kicked) her mammy and pa.

Old Melinda

My recorded references for this one include recordings by Mel Durham, Lynn "Chirps" Smith and The Rhythm Rats.

The choice of which part to call the A part and number of times through is a bit different in each version but this transcription follows the parts as played by Mel Durham - a wonderful old fiddler originally from Illinois - though he only plays the B part once.

Rattletrap

This one comes to me from the Easy Street and the Horseflies string bands, both of which list Joe Burchfield and the Roan Mountain Hilltoppers as their source. My favorite is the live recording of the Horseflies on the *Bound for Glory* radio program back around 1984.

During that show, in the intro to the tune, Judy Hymann (of the Horseflies) says they asked the Hilltoppers where they got the tune, and they said they "went up on a hill one day and it was given to them." Well, I'm just glad that it was given to them so they could give it to the Horseflies so I could learn it and give it to you! This one is related to the tune known as "Old Granny Rattletrap" by Uncle Am Stuart on the recording *The Revival of Uncle Am Stuart*.

And the CHORD/NOTE slide in measure 2 of the B part - D# or Eb? As written you just slide the chord and double stop notes up and back a half step. Whatever you want to call it, it's cool! Hold the notes and slip on up and back.

The B part is played 3 times through but it's only 4 measures long so comes out *short* and might feel a little weird as it goes back into the A part. I put the double tag on the end so you can use that instead of the "Final" measure to tag the tune like they do in that Easy Street recording! This one is a blast. A real banjo rattler! Fiddle rattl'r too.

69

Red Bird

Related to the old-time tune "Wake Up Susan" plus a third part. The difference is subtle but important. But then, those subtleties are what old time music is all about. Resist the urge to just play it that way.

71

Red Fox Waltz

Banjo - aDADE

Sometimes referred to as "The Texaco Star Waltz"
for those of you old enough to remember!

72

This tune runs long so some folks, like Charlie Walden, only play the B part once. Others, such as Cyril Stinnett, play it twice. BTW, they both have great recorded versions of this tune.

Reuben's Train

aka Train 45

O - l-d   Reu - ben had   a   train   went from   Eng - land   to   Spain   but he

could - n't   get a -   let - ter   from his   home.

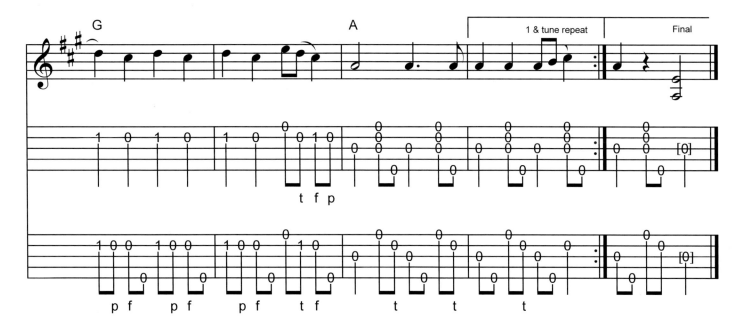

Alternate B-2 for Banjo players (not really a fiddle equivelent for this).

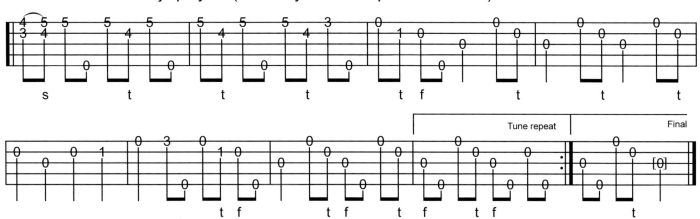

The words are similar to songs such as "500 Miles" or "100 Miles" but the history of this one is muddy to say the least, though this sure ain't the Peter, Paul and Mary melody! If you were singing the song you would probably follow the fiddle melody here though if playing and singing it as a solo banjo song you could easily insert the alternate B2 part as a little refrain. That alternate B2 is done in the style of Fred Cockerham from his version of "Train 45" adding an old railroad whistle effect in the break. A nice railroad style rhythm makes this one come alive as well.

Some verses:

(A1) Old Reuben had a train, went from England to Spain, but he couldn't get a letter from his home,
(A2) Oh, me, oh lord-y my no he couldn't get a letter from his home.

Should been in town when Reuben's train went down, you could hear that whistle blow 100 miles,
Oh me, oh my you could hear the whistle blow 100 miles

Cause me to weep, and it cause me to morn, cause me to leave my good ol home.
Oh me, oh lordy my, cause me to leave my good old home.

Ol Reuben made a train & he put it on a track, he ran it to the Lord knows where
Oh me, oh my ran it to the Lord knows where

Oh Reuben was killed on that C & O line, his poor body never was found
Oh, me, oh lordy my, his poor body never was found.

I got myself a blade, laid Reuben in the shade, I'm startin' me a graveyard of my own.
Oh, me, oh Lordy my, startin' me a graveyard of my own.

75

Rocky Mountain Goat

Check out versions of this tune by any of the old masters including Doc Roberts, Henry Reed, Lonnie Seymour, Mel Durham, Vernon Tilly or The Mississippi Sawyers. It's a great new standard to include in your jam repertoire, interesting but accessible.

Sadie

Banjo - aDADE

The key of D version

78

This is an unusual version of the tune with this name that I based on the playing of the Canote brothers and the Small Wonder String band. Jonathan Beckoff's playing is credited as well and there is even a video of him playing it online. It is pretty popular these days at Tucson jams.

Sail Away Ladies

Banjo - gDGBD

80

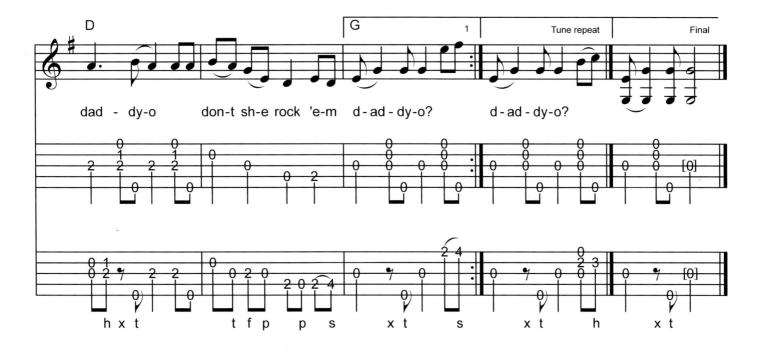

An oldie but a goodie! While it plays equally well in G or A, I wrote it here in G since that is a better vocal key for most folks than A would be.

There are so many good reference recordings for this tune I'd be hard pressed to name a favorite. How about looking up the old Highwoods String Band or Volo Bogtrotters' versions. They are both barn burners and great place to start!

Here are some good words most folks will recognize as a place to start.

(If) ever I get my new house done,
Sail away ladies, sail away
I'll give my old one to my son.
Sail away ladies, sail away.

Chorus:
Don't she rock 'em daddy-o? Don't she rock 'em daddy-o?
Don't she rock 'em daddy-o? Don't she rock 'em daddy-o?

Ain't no use to grieve and cry.
Sail away ladies, sail away
You'll be an angel, bye and bye.
Sail away ladies, sail away.

Come along, girls, and go with me.
Sail away ladies, sail away
We'll go back to Tennessee.
Sail away ladies, sail away.

Got me a letter from Shiloh Town.Sail away ladies, sail away
Said St. Louis is a' burning down. Sail away ladies, sail away.

I chew my tobacco and I spit my juice. Sail away ladies, sail away
I love my own daughter but it ain't no use. Sail away ladies, sail away.

81

Shady Grove

82

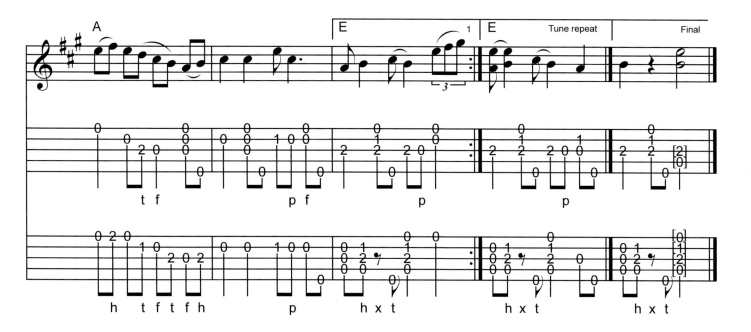

"Shady Grove" is a VERY old tune with many, many versions and recordings out there but this one is a version credited to fiddler *Pete Sutherland*. He considers himself the *re-creator* of this one and you can hear him play it on his Arm and Hammer String Band recording *Stay on the Farm*. If you can't find a copy, email Pete via his website (currently http://www.epactmusic.com/) to see if he can hook ya up. The only other recording of this version I have heard is by the Volo Bogtrotters – another of my favorite bands of the current old time world.

The verses are, as Pete says, "from here and there."

Verse (A1): Every time I go to town it's always dark and cloudy,
Every time I see that gal I always tell her "howdy."

Chorus (A2): Shady Grove my true love, Shady Grove I say,
Shady Grove my little love I'm bound to go away.

If I had a needle and thread as fine as I could sew
I'd sew that gal to my coattails and down the road we'd go.

Wish I was an apple, a hangin' on a tree
Every time that she'd pass by she'd take a bite of me.

The higher up the cherry tree, the sweeter are the cherries
The more you hug and kiss the girls, the sooner they will marry.

When I was a little boy, I wanted a Barlow knife
And now I want little Shady Grove to say she'll be my wife.

I wish I had a big fine horse, and corn to feed him on
With Shady Grove to stay at home, and feed him while I'm gone.

First time I seen Shady Grove, she's standing by the door
Shoes and stockin's in her hand, little bare feet on the floor.

Peaches in the summertime, apples in the fall
If I can't have my Shady Grove, I won't have none at all.

Sold a shirt to my true love, it's neither black nor brown
It's the color of the stormy skys before the rain comes down.

(John) Sharp's Hornpipe

Contrary to the title, this tune is obviously not a hornpipe, but a reel or breakdown. The chords here are what sound good to me and are how I would play this one. If you hear the old recordings of John Sharp's band playing it, you would swear it starts on the D (or IV chord) against the melody which plays in A. SO, you folks will have to decide for yourselves by experimenting and listening.

You can hear this tune played by John Sharp himself (and Band) on the County Recording Company's *Traditional Music of the Cumberland Plateau, Vol. 2.* Other references for this tune include recordings by The Horseflies, Ray Alden and Friends, and Old Buck.

Tippin' Back the Corn

© 1996 Jordan Wankoff – used by permission

Banjo - aEAC#E

This has become a session favorite almost overnight. I got it playing in a jam in Mountain View, Arkansas out front of the Poole family's Music Shop, aka *Mountain View Music*.

I like the A/B sequence of the parts as I have written but some folks play it the other way around. I asked Jordan (the composer) and he said he felt it works well either way.

The recorded references I have for this one so far are the recording by *Old Buck* (Riley Baugus, Emily Shaad, Debra Clifford and Sabra Guzman) who play the parts in the order written here, and another by Chirps Smith on his *Little Egypt* recording that reverses them. In our Tucson jams, I usually start it *here* but David likes to end it *there*.

While this tune was never copyrighted Jordan says he wrote it sometime in the mid-1990s. People can contact him at jwankoff@yahoo.com or they can find him on Facebook.

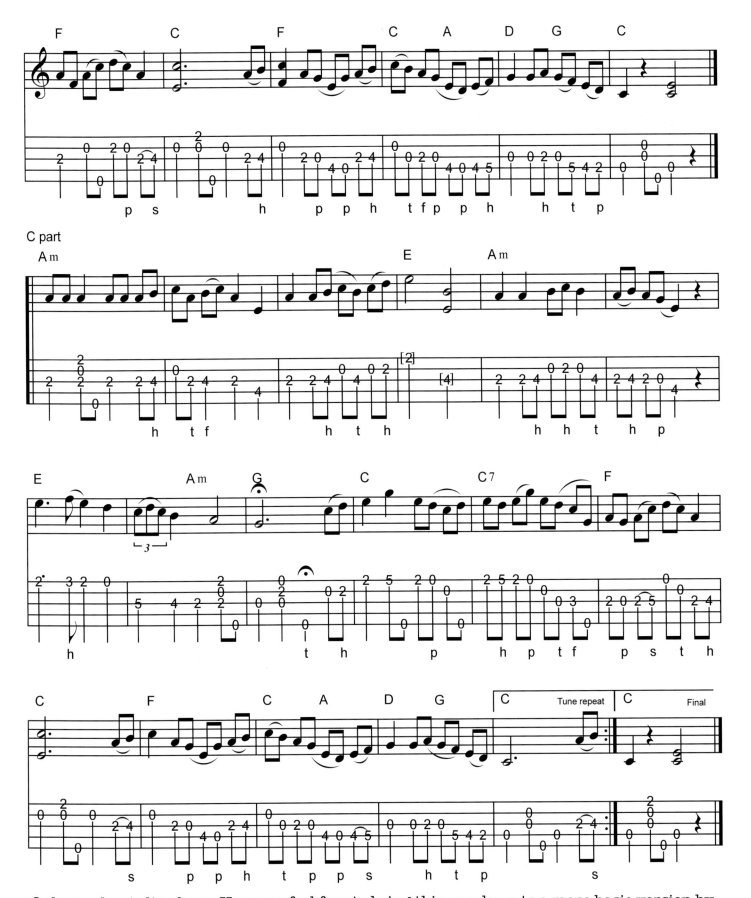

Only one banjo line here. You may feel free to bring this one down to a more basic version by playing the chord line with a simple *bum-pa-did-dy* double & drop thumb pattern if you like but either way, this one is gonna be a twister! Especially if you follow the suggested chords.

I'd check out Howdy Forrester (oldest source I could find) or Roger Cooper for a good recorded reference on this one. No drums please though. Ah well, who am I to say? Do as you do in your neck of the woods, just have a good time and *Play Nice!*

Woodchopper's Reel

For a recorded version of this one, I've got to go with the the *Hamilton Ironworks* album featuring fiddler extraordinaire John Hartford and clawhammer banjo master Bob Carlin. John has passed on but Bob is still thumpin' along.

PLEASE remember to *swing* this one! It is NOT a boring tune no matter who it comes from, but it can be if you let it. I've heard it happen and it is so, so sad to hear. With SO many notes this finger twister makes it all too easy to concentrate on getting the notes without the soul.

Final Thoughts

Okay, okay! I know you see it. Right there on the next page. *Over the Waterfall*! After all we talked about, after all of those *cool* tunes — what's the big idea?

Well, *Over the Waterfall* (or *OTWF* as it is sometimes *not* so endearingly known) is not a BAD tune, or even a particularly simple one, even if it is one of the more basic *everybody-plays-it* tunes. Perhaps it gets a bad rap because, since so many folks play it when they start out that by the time they get to where they play better and are ready for more advanced tunes, they are just tired of it. And SINCE it is such an oft played tune in beginner or basic jams, it can't be played in a very complicated form because the starting players need to be able to play it and keep up.

In other words, as the folks that usually play it are less accomplished players, the tune has to stay at a *basic* level. In *other*, other words, most folks have never really looked at this tune (and many other basic core tunes) with an eye (or is that *ear*) towards playing a more developed, interesting or even *extraordinary* version of Waterfalls, Soldiers or Ponies to find out what they COULD be.

Or perhaps you just HAVE to play that tune no matter what because, well, you just LIKE it. Then again, maybe you just want to see what can be done with it.

So, while we have agreed from the start that the premise of the book was to have more interesting tunes to play, I wondered what would happen if someone took the time to write out a more advanced version of this often played and overplayed tune. You know, *make* it interesting. Kind of take it *BEYOND* the waterfall we are used to. More like *Niagara* or even *Victoria* falls instead of *Chagrin* falls. I hear ya. *Now* you are wondering, "Dan, what can I do to make it more ... well, interesting? You know, take it *Beyond* the Waterfall or create *Over the Waterfall in a Barrel*?"

Okay okay, I understand so here is a very notey, more than too many notes, kind of slippery fall-off-the-rocks and *into, under AND over* the waterfall. NO, you don't have to play it this way and no, I don't know if I would, but I could. SO, I've added a lot of the notes you could possibly want. And you can play all the notes or you can take out the ones you don't like.

It's like I was told early in my days of playing: First you figure out how to play all the notes; then, you figure out which ones to leave out. And once you've done that, try reworking some of the other standards you have played over the years. Revisit the Soldier and the Pony. Travel back to Arkansas with those West Fork Gals. Gamble that Fortune and join me...

Beyond the Waterfall!

Play Nice!

Over the Waterfall

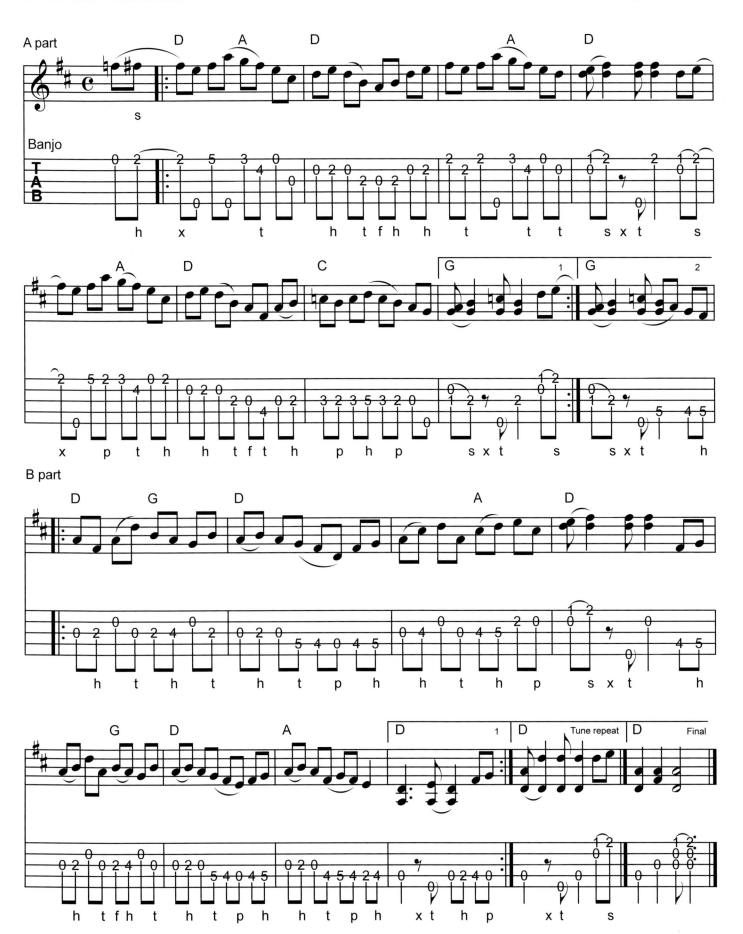

Banjo - aDADE

93

Other products by Dan Levenson

Books (Please note all books are Mel Bay publications)

Clawhammer Banjo From Scratch - This book starts at the beginning. You know, "This is a banjo," and goes from there. It takes you through all the basic techniques you'll need to play 12 common jam session tunes. All tunes are presented in double-thumb, drop-thumb & jam versions. With online audio.

Fiddle From Scratch - This book is an excellent introduction to the fiddle and old-time fiddle music. This book starts at the beginning. You know, "This is a fiddle". It takes you through all of the basic techniques you'll need to play the fiddle starting with holding and bowing the instrument. 15 common jam session tunes are presented, from basic melodies to full blown jam versions. It even introduces you to cross tuning - an important old time technique. With online audio.

First Lessons Folk Banjo - This one will teach you to play the banjo as a folk instrument to back up your singing, strum along with others, and even play the whole tune. Both down-picking and up-picking banjo styles are presented here, so you have a choice on how to play even if you've never played an instrument. With online audio.

First Lessons Clawhammer Banjo - Starting from the beginning clawhammer banjo basics and learning to read banjo music called tablature and moving quickly into technique, this will get you started the old time clawhammer way. Beginning in G tuning and introducing others, you can quickly start to play clawhammer style, even if you've never played any instrument at all. With online audio.

Old Time Festival Tunes for Clawhammer Banjo - Includes 117 old-time tunes with basic and advanced tab plus a standard notation line for other instruments. With online audio.

Old Time Festival Tunes for Fiddle & Mandolin - Another 117 old-time tunes with basic and advanced standard notation plus mandolin tab. With online audio.

Old Time Favorites for Clawhammer Banjo - Presents 62 old-time tunes with basic and advanced tab plus a standard notation line for other instruments. With online audio.

Old Time Favorites for Fiddle and Mandolin - Offers 62 old-time tunes with basic and advanced standard notation plus mandolin tab. With online audio.

Fred Cockerham and Tommy Jarrell - Clawhammer Banjo Masters - Co-written with Bob Carlin. Two tabs each of 23 tunes as a master played them, and as they are interpreted today. With online audio.

Wade Ward - Clawhammer Master - Co-written with Bob Carlin. Two tabs of each of 28 tunes both as the master played them, and as they are often interpreted today. With online audio.

Kyle Creed - Clawhammer Master - Co-written with Bob Carlin. Two tabs of each of 28 tunes both as the master played them, and as they are often interpreted today. With online audio.

Buzzard Banjo Clawhammer Style - 25 tunes tabbed out as played by Dan Levenson. Includes some basic instruction. With online audio.

Gospel Tunes for Clawhammer Banjo - Banjo tablature with standard notation of 27 Favorite Gospel tunes in an easy to play format. With online audio.

DVD - *Clawhammer Banjo From Scratch* - 2 DVD set - Instructional video - Clawhammer banjo players, start here! Disc 1 teaches the basics From Scratch through the double thumb "Spotted Pony" in double C. Disc 2 tunes you up to Double D and adds drop thumb, hammer-ons, pull-offs and more.

Recordings

Traveling Home (Buzzard 2005 CD) Banjo, fiddle, guitar and song solos and duos with Dan, Miss Jennifer and Rick Barron. Tunes: *Red-Haired Boy; Leaving Home; John Brown's Dream; Dry & Dusty; Camp Chase/Jenny Git Around; Texas Gals; John Lover's Gone; Texas; Milwaukee Blues; Kentucky John Henry; Lost Indian; Boatman; Durang's Hornpipe; Monkey on a Dogcart; Whistling Rufus; Sandy Boys; Arkansas Traveler/Mississippi Sawyer/Rock the Cradle Joe; Banjo Tramp.*

Barenaked Banjos (Buzzard 2002 CD) Solo banjo on 4 banjos! Tunes: *Katy Hill; Logan County Blues; Little Billie Wilson; Dr. Dr.; Texas Gals; Forked Deer; Staten Island; Liza Poor Gal; Johnny Don't Get Drunk; Rocky Pallet; Needlecase; Old Bell Cow; Fortune; Old Molly Hare/Rag Time Annie; Soldier's Joy; Billy in the Low Ground; Joke on the Puppy; Breaking Up Christmas; Whiskey Before Breakfast; Hangman's Reel; Duck River; Flying Indian; June Apple; Wild Horses at Stoney Point.*

Light of the Moon (Buzzard 2001 CD) Fiddle tunes to folk songs! Dan is joined on a few songs by guest musicians. Tunes: *June Apple; Cindy; Rushing the Pepper; Climbing the Golden Stairs; All God's Critters; Jaybird/Moses Hoe the Corn; Old Rip; The Fox; Rockin' Jenny; Soppin' the Gravy; Willow Waltz; Darlin' Corey; Buffalo Gals; Yellow Rose of Texas; Shelvin' Rock/Old Mother Flanagan; Snake River Reel; Hard Traveling; John Stenson's #2; Roseville Fair; Front Porch Waltz.*

New Frontier (Blue rose 1001 CD) All instrumental w/Dan Levenson on banjo, fiddle and guitar and Kim Murley on hammered dulcimer and Yang Qin (Chinese hammered dulcimer). Tunes: *Kitchen Girl/Growling Old Man, Grumbling Old Woman; Weaving Girl; Lullaby; Pachinko; Liza Poor Gal/Traveling Down the Road; Dance of the Yao People; Red Haired Boy; Duke of Kent's Waltz; Thunder on a Dry Day; Horse Race; Flying Indian; Dragon Boat; Mackinac Bats; Rosy Cloud Follows the Moon; Song of the Frontier; Cherry Blossom Waltz.*

Early Bird Special (Buzzard 1004 CD) Mostly instrumental (2 vocals) banjo, fiddle, guitar, and bass. Dan & The Boiled Buzzards Stringband. Tunes: *Smith's Reel; Beasties in the Sugar; Wooden Nickel; Brandywine/Three Forks of Reedy; The Engineers Don't Wave From the Train Anymore; Black Widow Romp; Young Guns and Miners; Boys Them Buzzards Are Flying; Lulu Loves Them Young; Bitter Creek; Lost Everything; Nixon's Farewell; Teabag Blues; Sadie at the Back Door/Waiting for Nancy; You Can't Get There From Here; Snake River Reel; Grey-Haired Dancing Girl; Cliff's Waltz.*

Eat at Joe's (Buzzard 1003 CD) All instrumental music played on banjo, fiddle, guitar, and bass. Dan & the Boiled Buzzards. Tunes: *Paddy on the Turnpike; John Brown's March/Waiting for the Federals; Snake River Reel; Hollow Poplar; Spotted Pony; Dinah/Wake Up Susan; Black Widow Romp; Katy Hill; Nixon's Farewell; Shady Grove; Spring in the Valley; Cuffy; The Year of Jubilo/Yellow Rose of Texas; Jimmy in the Swamp; Nixon's Farewell (w/double fiddles); Julianne Johnson; Tombigbee Waltz.*

Fine Dining (Buzzard 1002 CD) Mostly instrumental (2 vocals) banjo, harmonica, guitar, and bass. Dan plays with the Boiled Buzzards. Tunes: *Shuffle About; Little Dutch Girl; John Brown's Dream; Liza Jane; Goodbye Miss Liza; Booth Shot Lincoln; Briarpicker Brown; Monkey on a Dogcart; Fortune; Shenandoah Falls; Three Ponies; Jaybird; Forked Deer/Doctor Doctor; Leaving Home; Rock the Cradle Joe; Old Mother Flanagan; Santa Claus; Too Young to Marry; Roscoe; Stambaugh Waltz.*

Salt and Grease (Buzzard 1001 CD) Mostly instrumental (2 vocals) banjo, harmonica, guitar, and acoustic bass. This is The Boiled Buzzards' first album. Tunes: *Julianne Johnson; Three Thin Dimes; Durang's Hornpipe; Milwaukee Blues; Muddy Roads; Log Chain/Railroading Across the Rocky Mountains (Marmaduke's Hornpipe); Billy in the Lowground; Yellow Barber; Little Billy Wilson; Sandy Boys; Southtown; Rochester Schottische; Kansas City Reel; June Apple; Bull at the Wagon; Sally Ann Johnson; Nail That Catfish to a Tree; Icy Mountain; Benton's Dream; Sadie's Waltz.*

For up to date information and to order Dan's products, please go to
www.Clawdan.com

Beyond the Waterfall:
Extraordinary Tunes for Fiddle and Clawhammer Banjo

is written by:
Dan N. Levenson

Feel free to contact him through the
publisher or by e-mail at:
Clawdan@clawdan.com

You can also reach him on the web at:
http://www.Clawdan.com

Dan Levenson is a Southern Appalachian native who has grown up with the music of that region. Today he is considered a respected master teacher and performer of both the *Clawhammer banjo & Appalachian style fiddle. Banjo Newsletter*'s R.D. Lunceford describes Dan "as an interpreter, rather than a music re-creator". *Fiddler Magazine*'s Bob Buckingham described him as "an accomplished fiddler and ...one of the best clawhammer banjo players in the country." Ken Perlman has called him "The Johnny Appleseed of the Banjo".

Dan has won awards on both instruments including first place at the 2005 *Ohio Clawhammer Banjo Championship* and Grand Champion at the 2010 *Ajo, AZ Fiddle Contest.* He's made numerous recordings both with his band The Boiled Buzzards and as a solo artist.

Dan performs and teaches regularly throughout the country. He has taught clawhammer banjo, fiddle and stringband workshops at many music schools and camps including the *John C. Campbell Folk School, Mars Hill, Maryland Banjo Academy, The Ozark Folk Center* at Mountain View, AR, *Banjo Camp North , The Rolland Fiddle Camp* and Dan's own *Clawcamp* instructional weekend at his Appalachian homestead in Southeastern Ohio.

Dan is an author for Mel Bay publications. He is also a writer and editor for *Banjo Newsletter's* "Old Time Way". His books include *Clawhammer Banjo From Scratch; Old Time Fiddle From Scratch; First Lessons Clawhammer Banjo; First Lessons Folk Banjo; Old Time Festival Tunes* and *Old Time Favorites* (Clawhammer Banjo and Fiddle & Mandolin versions available for both titles); *Gospel Tunes for Clawhammer Banjo;* the *Clawhammer Banjo Masters* series with co-author Bob Carlin (Kyle Creed, Wade Ward and Fred Cockerham & Tommy Jarrell volumes available); and *Buzzard Banjo Clawhammer Style.*

To order Dan's books, recordings and for up to date information about Dan please go to
www.Clawdan.com